Department of Homeland Security
Office of Inspector General

Executive Summary

The Department of Homeland Security's mission includes law enforcement elements, which require the department, through its components, to manage various types of firearms. Our audit objective was to determine the efficacy of the Department of Homeland Security's management and oversight of its components to ensure that personnel were sufficiently safeguarding and controlling firearms.

The Department of Homeland Security, through its components, did not adequately safeguard and control its firearms. Components reported 289 firearms as lost during FYs 2006 through 2008. Although some reported losses were beyond the officers' control, most losses occurred because officers did not properly secure firearms. The department did not have a specific firearm policy and instead relied on the components to establish specific policies and procedures for managing, safeguarding, and controlling firearms. While some component policies were sufficient, personnel did not always follow them and the department did not require that independent third parties perform firearm inventories. Field offices did not always promptly report lost firearms to component headquarters or keep inventory records updated. Lost firearms pose serious risks to the public and law enforcement officers.

Based on the results of our audit we are making two recommendations to the department to improve controls over firearms. The Department of Homeland Security's Management Directorate and Office of the Chief Administrative Officer concurred with the recommendations. The components we reviewed in detail are already taking actions to correct the issues we identified.

Background

Between 2003 and 2007, the Government Accountability Office (GAO) and the Department of Justice Office of Inspector General assessed controls over firearms at 18 federal law enforcement agencies. The reports showed that these agencies faced similar challenges in safeguarding and controlling firearms and suffered losses of firearms under similar circumstances as the Department of Homeland Security (DHS). In some cases, DHS losses were fewer than other agencies, indicating that DHS may have stronger controls over its firearms.

To support its law enforcement mission DHS had over 188,548 firearms in its inventory as of July 2009. The components with firearms include:

- Customs and Border Protection (CBP);
- Federal Emergency Management Administration (FEMA);
- Federal Law Enforcement Training Center (FLETC);
- Immigration and Customs Enforcement (ICE);
- Science and Technology Directorate[1] (S&T);
- Transportation Security Administration (TSA);
- United States Coast Guard (USCG); and
- United States Secret Service (USSS).

Table 1 illustrates component inventories and table 2 illustrates the types of firearms carried by DHS law enforcement officers.

---

[1] The Science and Technology Directorate uses firearms solely in association with the testing mission of the Transportation Security Laboratory and does not issue side-arms to individuals.

Table 1: DHS Component Inventories as of July 2009[2]

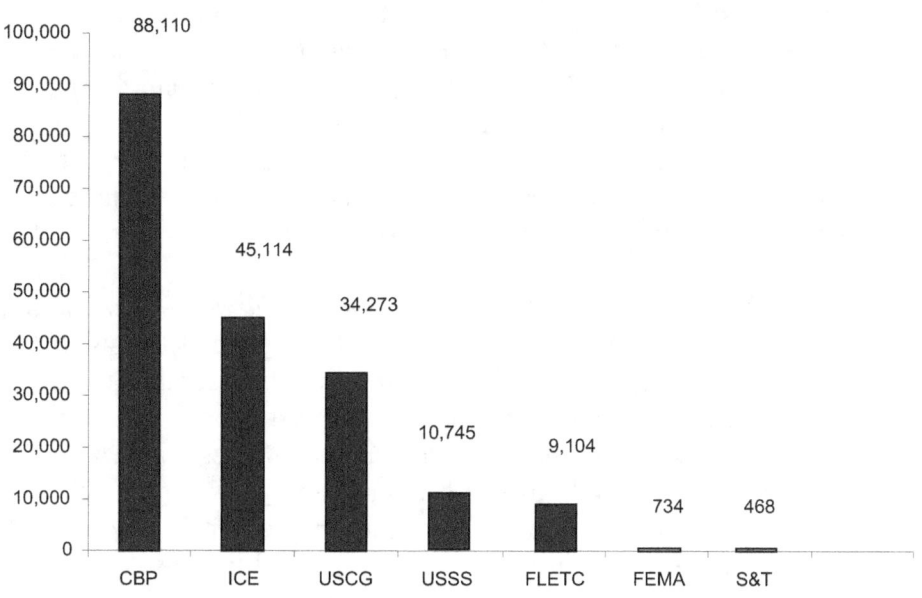

Component	Inventory
CBP	88,110
ICE	45,114
USCG	34,273
USSS	10,745
FLETC	9,104
FEMA	734
S&T	468

Table 2: Types of Weapons in Component Inventories

Handguns

Image courtesy of CBP

Semiautomatic / Automatic Weapons (M-4 Rifles)

Image courtesy of Colt Defense LLC

Shotguns

Image courtesy of Remington

---

[2] We did not include the number of firearms in TSA's inventory because this information is protected as Sensitive Security Information under 49 CFR 1520.5(b)(8)(ii). We also did not list the total number of firearms in DHS' inventory to protect TSA's Sensitive Security Information.

The Use of Force Policy Division at CBP and the National Firearms and Tactical Training Unit at ICE oversee their respective component firearms programs. CBP and ICE used the Firearms, Armor, and Credentials Tracking System (FACTS) to manage firearm inventories. CBP transferred its inventory data from the Firearms Inventory Tracking System to FACTS in April 2009. FACTS maintains information relating to individual firearms, such as the serial number, location, date of last inventory, assigned officer, and officer qualification scores.

In 1982, Congress established the *Federal Managers' Financial Integrity Act* (FMFIA) requiring executive agencies to establish and maintain controls that provide reasonable assurance that federal entities safeguard assets against waste, loss, unauthorized use, and misappropriation. The act also mandates that GAO's internal control standards serve as the framework for agencies to use in establishing and maintaining internal control systems. GAO internal control standards provide that in establishing internal controls, agencies should assess the risks associated with asset losses and establish control activities to help ensure those risks are addressed.

In addition to the FMFIA and GAO internal control standards, two other organizations issued advisory criteria addressing inventory controls. In June 1995, the Joint Financial Management Improvement Program addressed management's responsibility to provide guidelines for developing, documenting, and implementing physical controls to safeguard and provide accountability for inventory items. In August 1983, the Commission on Accreditation for Law Enforcement Agencies, Inc., an independent accrediting authority for law enforcement agencies, published accreditation standards that include procedures for inventory and property control. These inventory control requirements apply to sensitive property, such as firearms, to limit accessibility to authorized individuals and ensure accountability.

DHS Management Directive 0565, DHS Personal Property Management, provides a general description of controls for managing property and does not include controls over sensitive items, such as firearms.

We assessed the efficacy of DHS' management and oversight of its components to ensure that personnel were sufficiently safeguarding and controlling firearms. During our audit, we tested the accuracy of inventory records for 1,528 firearms, observed firearm storage procedures, and reviewed inventory policies and procedures at 6 CBP and 10 ICE field offices.

Results of Audit

The department's management and oversight of component safeguards and controls over firearms were not effective. A key reason that firearm controls were not sufficient was because DHS did not have specific firearms policies and procedures in place. Instead, DHS relied on its components to augment its general property management policies and procedures with specific guidance for safeguarding and controlling firearms. Although some component policies and procedures for safeguarding firearms were sufficient, personnel did not always follow them. Component personnel did not always sufficiently safeguard their firearms and, as a result, lost[3] a significant number of firearms between FY 2006 and FY 2008. Most of the losses occurred because law enforcement officers did not sufficiently secure firearms in their possession. The lost firearms created unnecessary risk to the public and law enforcement personnel; in some cases state and local law enforcement officials recovered lost DHS firearms from felons and gang members.

In addition, the department did not require independent third parties to perform annual firearm inventories, component field offices did not always promptly report lost and stolen firearms to component headquarters, and field offices did not keep inventory records updated. As a result, DHS could not ensure that components safeguarded and controlled firearms, or provided accountability over firearms.

During our audit, CBP and ICE initiated changes to their management and oversight of firearms to correct deficiencies we identified during this audit. Both components are reviewing or strengthening policy and procedures for safeguarding firearms and reporting lost firearms.

---

[3] Lost firearms are those no longer in the possession of the components; they include firearms that were lost or stolen.

Safeguarding Firearms

The department, through its components, did not adequately safeguard and control firearms. During FYs 2006 through 2008, DHS components reported 289 handguns, M-4 rifles, and shotguns as lost. CBP and ICE reported 243 (84%) of the 289 lost firearms. The remaining 46 lost firearms (16%) were reported by USCG (9), TSA (22), and USSS (15)[4].

When a law enforcement officer determines that a firearm is missing, CBP and ICE policies require that the officer send a memorandum reporting the loss, and a description of the situation surrounding that loss, to the supervisor. The supervisor forwards the notification of loss to the respective component headquarters personnel, who create a case file for the lost firearm. We reviewed 243 case files for firearms reported lost by CBP and ICE. For each case file, we determined the reason for the reported loss and evaluated those circumstances against the respective component's policies and procedures.

Lost Firearms

CBP and ICE reported 243 lost firearms during FYs 2006 through 2008. According to our analysis:

- 36 firearms (15%) were lost due to circumstances beyond the control of the officers. For example, CBP lost firearms when Hurricane Katrina made landfall and ICE lost a firearm during an assault on an officer.
- 28 firearms (about 11%) were lost even though officers stored them in lockboxes or safes.
- 179 firearms (74%) were lost because officers did not properly secure them.

Of the 179 firearms, CBP and ICE reported 59 (33%) firearms as lost and 120 (67%) firearms as stolen. Since the components' guidance did not provide a standard methodology for classifying and reporting lost firearms, officers tended to report a firearm as stolen rather than lost. This was due to a common perception among officers that reporting a stolen firearm was more acceptable

---

[4] According to Secret Service officials, 3 of the 15 firearms reported as lost or stolen between 2006 and 2008 were actually lost in the 2001 attack on the World Trade Center. The loss of these firearms was reported in 2008.

than reporting a lost firearm. Although CBP and ICE reported 120 firearms as stolen, our analysis showed that these firearms were lost (stolen) because officers left the firearms unsecured. All 179 losses may have been prevented had the officers properly safeguarded their firearms. For example, an officer left his firearm in the restroom of a fast food restaurant, and when he returned to retrieve it, it was gone. The case file listed this firearm as stolen; however, we believe that the firearm would not have been stolen had the officer exercised due diligence in safeguarding the firearm.

The following examples further demonstrate the inappropriate practices some officers used to store firearms in vehicles and residences:

- A CBP officer left a firearm unsecured in an idling vehicle in the parking lot of a convenience store. The vehicle and firearm were stolen while the officer was inside the store. A local law enforcement officer later recovered the firearm from a suspected gang member and drug smuggler.

- A CBP officer left a firearm on a toolbox in the bed of a truck, and the firearm fell off when the officer drove home. Law enforcement officials later recovered the firearm from an individual who resisted arrest and assaulted the arresting officer.

- An ICE officer left an M-4 rifle and a shotgun unsecured in a closet in his home; subsequently, both firearms were stolen during a burglary. State and federal law enforcement officers later recovered these firearms from a felon.

- An ICE officer left a firearm on the bumper of a vehicle, which fell off as the officer left his place of employment. A civilian found the firearm and turned it over to the local police.

Other CBP and ICE officers left firearms in places such as a fast food restaurant parking lot, a bowling alley, and a clothing store. Although our review focused on CBP and ICE, other components described similar incidents. For example, a TSA officer left a firearm in a lunch box on the front seat of an unlocked vehicle; the officer realized the firearm was stolen when he returned to the vehicle 2 days later. Officers may have prevented many of these losses had they exercised reasonable care when storing their firearms.

CBP and ICE officers lost 28 firearms even though they secured the firearms in lockboxes or safes. The components may have prevented these losses through more stringent policies and procedures. CBP policies and procedures for leaving a firearm in an unattended vehicle are inadequate and do not include requirements to secure the firearm to the vehicle. Although ICE policies and procedures for storing firearms in vehicles are more stringent, requiring officers to secure them to the vehicle with an ICE-approved safety-locking device, ICE does not require that its staff permanently secure the locking device to the vehicle. While using a safety-locking device is a good practice, the best way to protect firearms from theft is to store them in lockboxes properly mounted as recommended in the manufacturers' guidelines.

Storing Firearms at Field Offices

Law enforcement officers at field offices did not always use the locking devices provided by CBP and ICE to store their firearms in vehicles. We observed firearm storage procedures and verified 1,528 firearm serial numbers at 6 CBP and 10 ICE field offices. Officers stored 152 of the 1,528 firearms we examined in vehicles. Of the 152 firearms stored in vehicles, 58 (38%), were unsecured. CBP and ICE provided most officers with lockboxes and a locking cable to secure their firearms. However, in these 58 cases, the officers did not use the locking devices. In addition to the locking devices, some ICE facilities provided officers access to lockers to secure their firearms during working hours, as shown below:

Lockers provided for ICE officers to secure firearms – DHS-OIG Photo

Even though the officers had securing devices and access to these lockers, some officers chose to leave their firearms unsecured in their vehicles. The following examples and photos illustrate how some officers stored firearms in vehicles[5]:

- An ICE officer stored the keys for his assigned government-owned vehicle next to a windshield wiper blade. We observed the officer retrieve the keys, unlock the trunk, and reveal an unsecured firearm, body armor, and radio equipment. After our verification of the firearm serial number, the officer returned the keys to the windshield wiper blade.

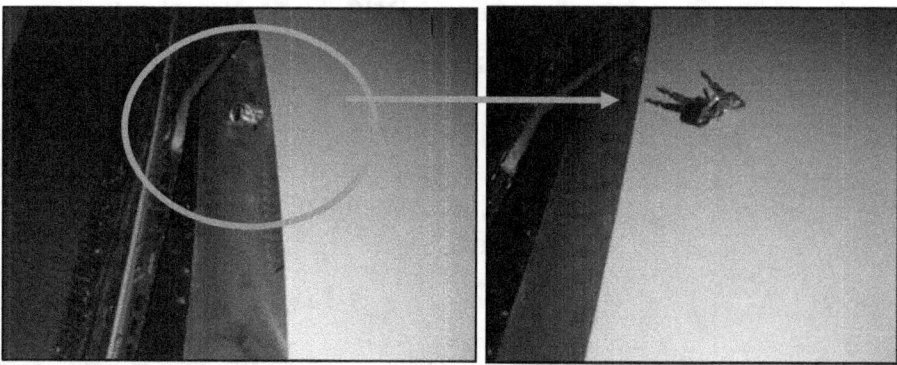

Keys to government- issued vehicle stored next to windshield wiper — DHS-OIG Photo

- CBP and ICE firearms instructors left firearms unsecured in vehicles. The firearms were stored in bags that were visible from the windows of the vehicles and not secured to the vehicles.
- Other CBP and ICE officers stored firearms in glove compartments and center consoles, under seats, and in various types of bags.

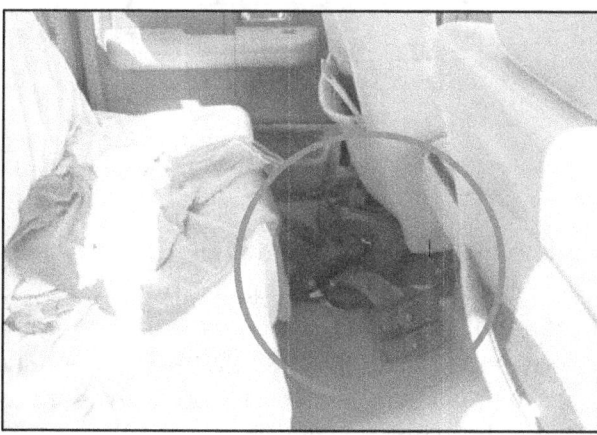

Firearm unsecured in duty belt in an officer's vehicle — DHS-OIG Photo

---

[5] We notified local supervisors of these issues as we identified them.

Recovered Firearms

According to CBP and ICE case files, 65 (27%) of the 243 lost firearms were recovered; of the 65 recovered firearms, 50 (77%) were recovered by the components or civilian organizations, and 15 (23%) were recovered by other law enforcement organizations. Although lost firearms account for a minor percentage of DHS' total firearms inventory, they pose serious risks to civilians and non-civilians alike. Local law enforcement organizations recovered 15 DHS firearms from felons, gang members, criminals, drug users, and teenagers. For example, law enforcement officers:

- Recovered a firearm from a suspected gang member. The suspect was driving a recreational vehicle with modified hidden compartments that had trace evidence of illegal drugs.

Firearm recovered with gang symbol etched on the barrel.

— Photo courtesy of the Lake City Police Department

- Recovered a lost firearm from an individual who was in possession of cocaine.
- Recovered a firearm from a drug dealer while executing a narcotics search warrant.

Reporting Lost Firearms

Although officers immediately reported the lost firearms to their supervisors and the National Crime Information Center[6] as required, officers did not always report lost firearms to the component headquarters in a timely manner. In some cases, it took nearly 3 years to report the loss to the component headquarters. According to the case files, CBP and ICE staff took an average of

---

[6] The National Crime Information Center is a computerized database for ready access by law enforcement agencies to assist in apprehending fugitives, locating missing persons, locating and returning stolen property, and protecting the law enforcement officers encountering the individuals described in the system.

about 2 months and 4 months, respectively, to report lost firearms to component headquarters, ranging from the day of loss to nearly 3 years after the loss. The reporting delays were due to incomplete reporting policies and procedures.

CBP and ICE have incomplete requirements for reporting lost and stolen firearms. Both of their policies and procedures state that when a firearm is lost or stolen the officer must report the loss or theft immediately or as soon as practicable to a supervisor. However, beyond the initial reporting, some critical reporting requirements are not stated. For example, CBP and ICE policies and procedures do not state the timeframes for reporting lost firearms to the National Crime Information Center. (See Appendix C for the table illustrating the incomplete reporting requirements.)

In addition, CBP operates under three inconsistent policies: the former Customs policy, the former Immigration and Naturalization Service policy, and the current ICE policy (only one CBP division follows the current ICE policy). Although ICE has only one policy, it does not address all the critical reporting requirements. Without consistent reporting requirements, the components and department cannot maintain visibility over firearms inventories.

Accounting Inventory Control

Independent third parties do not conduct annual firearms inventories at CBP and ICE. In addition, component personnel did not always enter some acceptances and transfers into the inventory system promptly. CBP and ICE rely on law enforcement personnel and their supervisors to conduct inventories. The delays in acceptances and transfers occurred because CBP and ICE do not have policies and procedures addressing the timelines for these actions. As a result, the inventories were not always accurate or updated.

<u>Annual Inventory</u>

Independent third parties do not conduct annual inventories of firearms at CBP and ICE. CBP and ICE guidance does require that field office personnel conduct annual inventories to ensure the completeness and accuracy of the firearms inventory information within the inventory system. The policy requires personnel to complete an annual inventory over a 30-day period. The officer assigned the firearm is responsible for verifying the serial number and other pertinent information, and entering the data into FACTS. Subsequently, the officer's supervisor is responsible for ensuring that the officer appropriately inventoried the correct firearm through visual inspection of the officer's firearm and verification of the information entered into FACTS. We identified six cases of lost firearms where supervisors did not perform a visual inspection; however, they still verified the firearm within the inventory system over several years.[7] The following history of one of these six lost CBP firearms illustrates this annual inventory control weakness:

- September 2004 – An officer's firearm was stolen from his vehicle but the loss was not recorded in the FACTS inventory system.

- August 2005 – Another officer recorded in FACTS that the stolen firearm was in his possession.

- September 2005 – This officer's supervisor affirmed information about this firearm in FACTS.

- December 2006 – A third officer entered the firearm information into FACTS (as if it were not lost).

- December 2006 – This officer's supervisor affirmed the firearm information in FACTS.

- August 2007 – The third officer again entered firearm information into FACTS (as if it were not lost) as part of the annual inventory process.

- September 2007 – Supervisor verified this firearm information in FACTS.

As of 2009, CBP and ICE require supervisors to affirm, within the inventory system, that they visually verified the serial numbers of officers' firearms during the annual inventory. Although this is a reasonable control, affirmations do not replace inventories performed by independent third parties.

Acceptances and Transfers

Component personnel did not always promptly update acceptances of firearms and transfers of officers' firearms in the inventory system. Component policies and procedures do not address the

---

[7] We referred these six cases to the CBP Office of Internal Affairs for further review.

timely inputting of acceptances and transfers. Acceptances occur to document the receipt of new firearms. Transfers occur to document a change in an officer's duty station or a change in status of an issued firearm. As a result, the components did not always maintain up-to-date inventory records, which reduced accountability in the management of firearms.

Our review of CBP and ICE resulted in 29 inventory control inaccuracies (22 at CBP and 7 at ICE). For example:

- A CBP facility did not include three firearms issued to the facility in their inventory system. CBP updated the inventory when we pointed out the discrepancy.

- An ICE officer transferred from one office to another but the officer's information, including inventory data for his firearm, did not transfer to the new inventory records for several weeks. ICE updated the inventory records when we pointed out the discrepancy.

Actions Taken by CBP and ICE

CBP is developing and implementing changes in its management and oversight of firearms to improve firearms accountability and to correct deficiencies identified during our audit. To correct the deficiencies, CBP initiated the following actions:

- Transitioned to a web-based firearms accountability system in April 2009.
- Created a monthly review process of lost firearms to improve its oversight and accountability.
- Developed a unified Use of Force Policy, which is currently in the staffing and approval process.
- Reviewed policies and procedures regarding the safeguarding and controlling of firearms in vehicles to determine if they are sufficient.
- Utilized the CBP*net* to remind law enforcement personnel of the reporting requirements for lost, stolen, or missing firearms.
- Developed a presentation that addresses the proper methods for safeguarding and controlling firearms, which CBP plans to use annually.

ICE initiated changes in its management and oversight of firearms to correct deficiencies identified during our audit. To correct the deficiencies, ICE initiated the following actions:

- Developed methods to promote firearms security awareness through policy and procedure clarifications, and posters to reinforce firearms storage requirements.
- Drafted a memorandum to remind all ICE program office directors of their responsibility to ensure that armed personnel safeguard all issued or approved personally owned firearms in accordance with ICE policies and procedures.
- Drafted a second memorandum to provide supplementary guidance regarding the processes officers should use to report lost and stolen firearms and the required documentation for transfer and receipt of firearms.
- Recommended that its Office of Professional Responsibility Management Inspection Unit expand the scope of their firearms field audits to include a review of the individual officers' storage practices.

Conclusion

The prescribed guidance for DHS and the augmented guidance developed by the components are incomplete and inconsistent to ensure that firearms are protected against loss and unauthorized use. By developing standard policies and procedures, DHS could reduce the number of lost firearms and improve its accountability over its firearm inventory.

Recommendations

We recommend that the Undersecretary for Management:

Recommendation #1: Develop department-wide policies and procedures for safeguarding and controlling firearms. At a minimum, these policies and procedures should include:

a. Requirements for properly securing firearms, including a requirement to use properly mounted lockboxes.

b. Timelines for recording acceptances and transfers in the inventory system.

c. Requirements for reporting lost firearms, including classification of lost versus stolen, and timelines for reporting lost firearms to supervisors, local law enforcement, the National Crime Information Center, and component headquarters.

    d.   Inventory procedures that include having an independent third party observe annual inventories.

Recommendation #2: Assess firearm security equipment needs for each officer assigned a firearm, issue security equipment as needed, and reaffirm to each officer the requirement to always properly secure firearms.

Management Comments and OIG Analysis

DHS provided comments to our draft report, concurring with both recommendations. Below is a summary of the written response from DHS and our analysis of the response. A copy of the Undersecretary of Management's response, in its entirety, appears in Appendix B.

DHS Response to Recommendation #1: The Undersecretary of Management concurred with our recommendation and said that the Office of the Chief Administrative Officer (OCAO) has begun a complete revision of the DHS Property Management policy directive. Key controls addressed within the DHS Property Management policy directive will include the proper storage of weapons; recording and updating firearms inventory; classification of lost and stolen, and timeliness for reporting lost or stolen firearms; and proper inventory procedures.

OIG Evaluation: This recommendation is resolved, but remains open pending confirmation that the DHS implemented these key controls and that the key controls address the recommendation. Developing effective policies and procedures will assist in mitigating the risk of lost firearms.

DHS Response to Recommendation #2: DHS concurred with our recommendation. The OCAO will review the component's requirements for firearm security equipment and collaborate with them to determine the effectiveness of their current equipment. In addition, the OCAO will require that all components conduct annual firearm security requirements awareness training.

OIG Evaluation: This recommendation is resolved, but remains open pending confirmation that DHS implemented these policies and procedures and that the policies and procedures appropriately address the recommendation. Developing effective policies and procedures will assist in mitigating risks associated with maintaining security over firearms.

This report provides the results of our work to determine the efficacy of DHS management and oversight of component safeguards and controls over firearms. To achieve our objectives we:

- Interviewed DHS officials regarding management of personal property, specifically firearms, and the related policies and procedures for DHS and the components;

- Reviewed DHS organizational charts, and manuals for tracking systems and firearms inventories;

- Reviewed case files and data for the components' lost firearms from FYs 2006 through 2008;

- Contacted law enforcement agencies and the Federal Bureau of Investigation to obtain information regarding the circumstances surrounding the recovery of lost firearms;

- Interviewed officers, observed the storage of firearms, and physically verified that serial numbers and the make and model of the officers' firearms matched the inventory listing provided to us by CBP and ICE;

- Conducted fieldwork at 16 CBP and ICE locations, verified the serial numbers for 1,528 issued firearms, and observed storage practices for 152 firearms;

- Reviewed prior audit reports regarding DHS, the components, and other federal agencies that have armed law enforcement officers; and

- Assessed the reliability and validity of data provided by the components by performing a physical verification of inventory data and comparing relevant data from multiple sources.

We conducted our audit between February and July 2009 under the authority of the *Inspector General Act of 1978*, as amended, and according to generally accepted government auditing standards. Those standards require that we plan and perform the audit to obtain sufficient, appropriate evidence to provide a reasonable basis for our findings and conclusions based on our audit objectives. We believe that the evidence obtained provides a reasonable basis for our findings and conclusions based on our audit objectives.

U.S. Department of Homeland Security
Washington, DC 20528

DEC 1 1 2009

Homeland Security

MEMORANDUM FOR: Anne L. Richards
                    Assistant Inspector General for Audits

FROM: Elaine C. Duke
                    Under Secretary for Management

SUBJECT: Draft Report: DHS Controls Over Firearms

Thank you for the opportunity to respond to the findings and recommendations in the Office of Inspector General (OIG) draft report titled, "DHS Controls Over Firearms" which was transmitted via your memorandum dated October 23, 2009. The report addresses the efficacy of the Department of Homeland Security's management and oversight of its Components to ensure that personnel are sufficiently safeguarding and controlling firearms.

The Management Directorate and the Office of the Chief Administrative Officer (OCAO) acknowledge the importance of effective controls over firearms and other sensitive assets and we are committed to improving current Department-wide policies and procedures, as well as strengthening OCAO oversight of the property management program throughout the Department. OCAO worked with each of the Components that was audited (Customs and Border Protection [CBP], Immigration and Customs Enforcement [ICE], and Transportation Security Administration [TSA]) in order to identify corrective actions and any concerns relative to the draft report. We believe this demonstrates our commitment to the Secretary's One DHS initiative and that it will help improve management oversight of a DHS-wide program.

The draft audit report recommendations and our responses and comments follow:

Recommendation #1: Develop department-wide policies and procedures for safeguarding and controlling firearms. At a minimum, these policies and procedures should include:

> **a. Requirements for properly securing firearms, including a requirement to use properly mounted lockboxes.**

We concur with this recommendation. OCAO has begun a complete revision of the DHS Property Management policy directive. In addition, OCAO will initiate a comprehensive review of current component requirements for securing firearms and other sensitive assets with the goal of identifying best practices to secure, safeguard and control these assets. Several key controls will be addressed in the department-wide policies and procedures including:

- Proper storage of weapons;
- Ensuring accountability for safeguarding and controlling firearms;

- Standard training for Component level personnel who have responsibility for firearms to raise awareness of the accountability aspects of DHS firearms controls;
- Requirements for investigation when determinations are made that individuals do not follow accountability procedures.

b. Timelines for recording acceptances and transfers in the inventory system.

We concur with this recommendation. It should be noted that of all the Components that use and store weapons, only two (CBP and ICE) use the same inventory system to manage their weapons. However, OCAO will initiate DHS-wide inventory controls to ensure written policies and procedures are implemented to require accurate and timely firearms property records and systems are maintained. The policies and procedures will include specific requirements to:

- Record firearms upon receipt;
- Update firearms inventory data upon removal of firearms from agency for losses and disposals;
- Update firearms inventory data to reflect discrepancies after on-hand inventory counts.

c. Requirements for reporting lost firearms, including classification of lost versus stolen, and timelines for reporting lost firearms to supervisors, local law enforcement, the National Crime Information Center, and component headquarters.

We concur with this recommendation. OCAO has initiated a review of the current definitions and use of these terms. A consistent DHS-wide policy regarding the classification of lost and stolen, and the timelines for reporting lost or stolen firearms, will be included in the revised Property Management policy directive and distributed throughout the Department.

d. Inventory procedures that include having an independent third party observe annual inventories.

We concur with this recommendation. Due to the diverse nature of the DHS Component operations, third party participation in the annual inventories may be achieved in a variety of different ways. OCAO will review current component inventory policies and procedures and issue instructions regarding proper inventory procedures.

Recommendation #2: Assess firearm security equipment needs for each officer assigned a firearm, issue security equipment as needed, and reaffirm to each officer the requirement to always properly secure firearms.

We concur with this recommendation. OCAO will review Components' requirements for firearm security equipment and collaborate with them to determine the effectiveness of their current equipment. OCAO will require that all components conduct annual firearm security requirements awareness training for all personnel issued firearms. The training will emphasize the importance of properly securing firearms and the risks associated with failing to maintain effective custody of DHS issued firearms.

As noted in the draft report, the Components that were audited took immediate and substantive actions to correct noted deficiencies and to improve the overall management of their firearms. OCAO has initiated action to revise its policies and procedures, with the expectation that a new policy directive will be issued by the spring of 2010. Concurrent with that effort, OCAO will develop a Management Action plan by December 30, 2009, to identify remaining actions, milestones and resource requirements.

	CBP Policies		ICE Policy
Critical Reporting Steps	**Customs Policy**	**Immigration and Naturalization Service Policy**	**ICE Interim Policy**
Report lost firearm to supervisor	Immediately	As soon as practical	Immediately
Report lost firearm to local law enforcement	Not stated	As soon as possible from supervisor	Not required
Report lost firearm to component headquarters	No timeframe	Within 24 hours	Immediately from supervisor
Report lost firearm to National Crime Information Center	No timeframe	Not stated	No timeframe
Memo prepared by employee	Not stated	Within 48 hours	Within 48 hours
Report to Joint Intake Center (JIC)	Not stated	Not stated	Not stated
Significant Incident Report	Not stated	Within 24 hours	Not stated
Report of survey	No timeframe	No timeframe	Not stated
CBP - Internal Affairs	No timeframe	Within 24 hours by HQs	Not applicable
ICE - Office of Professional Responsibility	Not applicable	Not applicable	As soon as practicable from supervisor

Linda Howard, Director
Sean Pettersen, Audit Manager
David DeHaven, Auditor-in-Charge
Lindsay Cabral, Auditor
Brian Blaha, Auditor
Victoria Phan, Program Analyst
Kevin King, Program Analyst
Joseph Faulk, Program Analyst
Lisa Vonder Haar, Desk Officer

Department of Homeland Security

Secretary
Deputy Secretary
Chief of Staff for Operations
Chief of Staff for Policy
General Counsel
Executive Secretariat
Director, GAO/OIG Liaison Office
Assistant Secretary for Office of Policy
Assistant Secretary for Office of Public Affairs
Assistant Secretary for Office of Legislative Affairs
Under Secretary, Management
DHS Audit Liaison
Acting Commissioner, CBP
CBP Audit Liaison
Assistant Secretary, ICE
ICE Audit Liaison
Acting Administrator, TSA
TSA Audit Liaison
Administrator, FEMA
FEMA Audit Liaison
Director, FLETC
FLETC Audit Liaison
Commandant, USCG
USCG Audit Liaison
Director, USSS
USSS Audit Liaison
Acting Under Secretary, S&T
S&T Audit Liaison

Office of Management and Budget

Chief, Homeland Security Branch
DHS OIG Budget Examiner

Congress

Congressional Oversight and Appropriations Committees, as
appropriate